To Live Is Christ

To Live Is Christ

by
John MacArthur, Jr.

MOODY PRESS
CHICAGO

© 1990 by
JOHN F. MACARTHUR, JR.

All rights reserved. No part of this book may be reproduced in any form without permission in writing from the publisher, except in the case of brief quotations embodied in critical articles or reviews.

All Scripture quotations, unless noted otherwise, are from the *New American Standard Bible*, © 1960, 1962, 1963, 1968, 1971, 1972, 1973, 1975, and 1977 by The Lockman Foundation, and are used by permission.

ISBN: 0-8024-5370-8

1 2 3 4 5 6 Printing/LC/Year 94 93 92 91 90

Printed in the United States of America

Contents

1. Joy in Spite of Trouble — 7
   Tape GC 50-7—Philippians 1:12-14

2. Joy in Spite of Detractors — 21
   Tape GC 50-8—Philippians 1:15-18

3. Joy in Spite of Death — 35
   Tape GC 50-9—Philippians 1:19-21

4. Joy in Spite of the Flesh — 47
   Tape GC 50-10—Philippians 1:22-26

   Scripture Index — 59

   Topical Index — 63

These Bible studies are taken from messages delivered by Pastor-Teacher John MacArthur, Jr., at Grace Community Church in Sun Valley, California. The recorded messages themselves may be purchased as a series or individually. Please request the current price list by writing to:

"GRACE TO YOU"
P.O. Box 4000
Panorama City, CA 91412

Or call the following toll-free number:
1-800-55-GRACE

1
Joy in Spite of Trouble

Outline

Introduction
A. The Believer's Joy Amidst Difficulties
B. Paul's Joy Amidst Difficulties
   1. His journey to Rome
   2. His house arrest
   3. His response to the Philippians

Lesson
I. Joy in Spite of Trouble (vv. 12-14)
   A. The Advance of Christ's Cause Outside the Church (v. 13)
      1. Paul's ministry among the guard
      2. Paul's ministry to the city
   B. The Advance of Christ's Cause Inside the Church (v. 14)

Conclusion

Introduction

The theme of Philippians 1:12-26 is joy in ministry. The keynote is Paul's declaration "I rejoice, yes, and I will rejoice" (v. 18). He wrote that statement in the midst of difficult circumstances. Yet in spite of the difficulties, Paul rejoiced in the ministry God had given him.

   A. The Believer's Joy Amidst Difficulties

   A believer's spiritual maturity can be measured by what it takes to steal his joy. Joy is a fruit of a Spirit-controlled life

(Gal. 5:22). We are to rejoice always (Phil. 4:4; 1 Thess. 5:16). In all circumstances the Spirit of God produces joy, so there ought not to be any time when we're not rejoicing in some way.

Although we should not allow circumstances to make us sullen, bitter, or negative, the one thing that will rob our joy is sin. Nothing short of sin should steal our joy. But change, confusion, trials, attacks, unmet desires, conflict, and strained relationships can throw us off balance and rob us of our joy if we're not careful. Then we cry out like the psalmist, "Restore to me the joy of Thy salvation" (Ps. 51:12).

We ought to expect trouble. Jesus said, "In the world you [will] have tribulation" (John 16:33). The apostle James said, "Consider it all joy . . . when you encounter various trials, knowing that the testing of your faith produces endurance" (James 1:2-3). God has His own profound purpose in our afflictions, but He never wants to take away our joy. To maintain joy we must adopt God's perspective regarding our trials. When we yield to the working of His Spirit in our lives, our difficulties will not overwhelm us.

B. Paul's Joy Amidst Difficulties

The apostle Paul seems almost larger than life because his joy knew no bounds. Reading through his letters, one could rightly assume that the greater the trial Paul faced, the greater his joy. His life was a living illustration of severe affliction mingled with supreme joy.

Paul was in Rome when he wrote to the Philippians, which is exactly where he wanted to be for many years (Rom. 15:23). He had written the Roman church that he had wanted to minister to them (1:11) and perhaps use Rome as a base from which to reach out to Spain (15:24).

But when Paul wrote to the Philippians, his circumstances were not in accord with what he had planned. He told the Romans of his desire to "have a prosperous journey by the will of God to come to [them]" (Rom. 1:10; KJV*). But in-

*King James Version.

stead he came to Rome in chains as a prisoner after being shipwrecked.

1. His journey to Rome

Acts 21-28 explains how Paul ended up in Rome. After his third missionary journey he returned to Jerusalem. To affirm he was still living in obedience to the law, he went to the Temple to participate in a ceremony. There he was accused of teaching against the law and violating the Temple and was attacked by a mob. He might have been killed had he not been rescued by Roman soldiers. They kept him in custody to protect him from his Jewish enemies.

As time passed, Paul became a point of contention between the Jewish and Roman authorities. Hearings before Governors Festus and Felix and an audience with King Agrippa brought no disposition of Paul's case. As a result, he languished for two years as a prisoner in Caesarea (where the Roman army was garrisoned). Eventually he appealed to Caesar and was dispatched by ship to Rome.

In Rome he spent another two years in prison (Acts 28:30). During that time he wrote what are known as the prison epistles, which include Philippians. He was given an initial opportunity to defend himself (perhaps alluded to in Philippians 1:7). At that time he probably spoke of his belief in Christ and his calling to preach the gospel. The Roman emperor at the time was Nero, so when Paul wrote to the Philippians, he was waiting for Nero to make up his mind regarding his case. Months may have passed while he awaited word of his release or execution.

2. His house arrest

The conditions of Paul's imprisonment were unusual. Acts 28:16 says, "When we entered Rome, Paul was allowed to stay by himself, with the soldier who was guarding him." He was not put in a prison with other criminals, for he had not committed any crime against Roman law. The Roman authorities probably realized there was no real criminal charge against Paul, yet because they could not release him before his case was adjudicated, they allowed him to be a private prisoner in his own quarters.

Paul was under constant guard. Verse 20 records his saying to Jewish leaders in Rome, "I requested to see you and to speak with you, for I am wearing this chain for the sake of the hope of Israel." The Roman government was sufficiently anxious about Paul that they kept him chained to a guard twenty-four hours a day. Roman custom provided for a change in guard every six hours, so Paul would have had four different men chained to him during the course of a day.

Nevertheless, Paul had many freedoms. He was allowed to see visitors (vv. 17, 23) and stay in a private residence (v. 30). He was allowed to preach and teach, and may have been allowed to leave for those purposes (vv. 30-31). The sphere of his preaching and teaching was essentially unhindered and included a captive audience—the Roman soldiers chained to him.

Yet that was a far cry from the freedom he previously enjoyed as he journeyed throughout a large part of the Roman Empire, founding and strengthening churches and training leaders. He was always on the move to realize his apostolic commission to the greatest extent possible. He continued to seek to fulfill his commission even though he was imprisoned in Rome. Yet he did not have the solitude that a man of God craves for his personal worship. Even in the little tasks of life he knew no privacy. Sleeping, writing, eating—in everything he had to endure the presence of the soldier he was chained to.

3. His response to the Philippians

The Philippians hadn't heard from Paul in a long time, yet by some means had been made aware that he was imprisoned at Rome. They loved him deeply and had always been compassionate and sympathetic toward him. So they were concerned about him and sent Epaphroditus to Rome to seek the answer to two questions: What was Paul's condition, and what was the condition of the gospel? They also sent along a monetary gift (Phil. 4:18-19) and commissioned Epaphroditus to help Paul as a loyal friend and companion (2:25-30).

Paul wrote to the Philippians to answer their questions. Paul's letter is full of joy and rejoicing because, in spite his circumstances, the gospel was going forward, and he had joy in his ministry. He didn't want the Philippians to worry needlessly about him, so he emphasized his joy throughout his letter to them.

a) Philippians 1:3-4—"I thank my God in all my remembrance of you, always offering prayer with joy in my every prayer for you all."

b) Philippians 2:17—"I rejoice and share my joy with you all."

c) Philippians 3:1—"Rejoice in the Lord."

d) Philippians 4:4—"Rejoice in the Lord always; again I will say, rejoice!"

Paul's joy was unrelated to his circumstances. If his joy had been tied to pleasures on earth, possessions, freedom, prestige, outward success, or a good reputation, he wouldn't have had any joy. Paul's joy was centered on his ministry and was indifferent toward all other things. He had joy in spite of trouble as long as Christ's cause was advanced. He had joy in spite of detractors as long as Christ's name was proclaimed. He had joy in spite of death as long as Christ was exalted. And he had joy in spite of the flesh as long as Christ's church was assisted.

Lesson

I. JOY IN SPITE OF TROUBLE (vv. 12-14)

"Now I want you to know, brethren, that my circumstances have turned out for the greater progress of the gospel, so that my imprisonment in the cause of Christ has become well known throughout the whole praetorian guard and to everyone else, and that most of the brethren, trusting in the Lord because of my imprisonment, have far more courage to speak the word of God without fear."

Paul had joy in spite of trouble. Even though he was in chains he rejoiced because he knew Christ's cause was progressing. That's in contrast to what we might think. Because of Paul's circumstances, it would be natural to assume his ministry had been totally crippled.

When Paul said, "I want you to know," he was using a phrase often used in ancient letters. Today we might write, "I want you to understand this," and we would be saying much the same thing Paul meant. The phrase is significant for two reasons: Paul was pointing to the importance of what he was about to write, and he was signaling that it could be easily misunderstood and therefore needed to be read carefully. It is a positive way of restating the phrase "I do not want you to be unaware" (Rom. 1:13; 1 Cor. 10:1; 12:1; 1 Thess. 4:13). The Philippians might have thought his imprisonment was a terrible thing, but Paul wanted them to understand it was just the opposite.

Paul called the Philippians "brethren"—a term of endearment used three other times in this epistle (3:1, 13; 4:1). It expresses the intimate fellowship that existed between Paul and the Philippian church. They were dear friends bonded in love as children of God. It was important to Paul that his dear brethren know that his circumstances, rather than hindering the gospel, had actually advanced it.

Paul knew that God had worked out a far better plan than he could have on his own. His ministry had not been shut down but expanded. The *New American Standard* translates verse 12 to read, "For the greater progress." A better translation would be "Rather, for the progress," which better reflects the meaning of the Greek text. Paul was emphasizing that things had turned out different from what one might have expected.

What Makes You Tick?

The progress of the gospel was the passion of Paul's life. How about you—what motivates you, sucks up your energy, dominates your time, makes you tick? It was of little consequence to Paul what happened to his own body or career. In Acts 20:24 we find him saying, "I do not consider my life of any account as dear to myself, in order that I may finish my course, and the ministry which I received from the Lord Jesus." Life, possessions, clothes, recognition, reputation, and prestige were all yielded up to one goal: "To testify solemnly of the gospel of the grace of God" (v. 24). To the Roman church Paul wrote, "I am eager to preach the gospel to you also who are in Rome" (Rom. 1:15). In 1 Corinthians 9:16 he said, "Woe is me if I do not preach the gospel." Paul was driven to see the progress of the gospel—what a model for every Christian! Are you that kind of person?

The Greek word translated "progress" (*prokopē*) refers to forward movement in spite of obstacles, dangers, and distractions. Commentator William Barclay said it was "specially used for the progress of an army or an expedition. It is the noun from the verb *prokoptein*, which means to cut down in advance. It is the verb which is used for cutting away the trees and the undergrowth, and removing the barriers which would hinder the progress of an army" (*The Letters to the Philippians, Colossians, and Thessalonians*, rev. ed. [Philadelphia: Westminster, 1975], p. 20). The chief obstacle for Paul was his imprisonment, but that proved to be no obstacle to the advancement of the gospel.

"The gospel" refers to the message of salvation. It is mentioned in verses 5, 7, 12, 16, and 27. That repetition shows the extent to which the gospel was on his heart. He lived to preach and advance it. And he had learned that every effort to stop the message of Christ only ended up furthering it.

A. The Advance of Christ's Cause Outside the Church (v. 13)

"My imprisonment in the cause of Christ has become well known throughout the whole praetorian guard and to everyone else."

Paul always saw himself as a prisoner because of Christ—never because of crime. He was in chains because he believed in, preached, and represented Jesus Christ.

Acts 28:20 says that Paul wore a chain, and in Ephesians 6:20 Paul speaks of himself as "an ambassador in chains." The usual Greek word for a prisoner's bonds is *desmos* (e.g., Acts 26:29). But in the above two instances, Paul's bonds are described as *halusis*—a short chain attached to the wrist of a prisoner and his guard. That was the kind of chain that bound Paul to his guard twenty-four hours a day. Escape was impossible and privacy nonexistent.

1. Paul's ministry among the guard

> The result of such close confinement was that the cause of Christ had "become well known throughout the whole praetorian guard." They were the men chained to Paul night and day. From the point of view of the Roman government, Paul was a captive chained to a Roman guard. But from Paul's point of view, the Roman guards were captives chained to him! What an opportunity to evangelize! Far from its being a burdensome condition, Paul had been given the opportunity to witness for Christ to each guard assigned to him, six hours at a stretch. Perhaps Christians in Rome had been praying for the opportunity to reach Caesar's household and the elite praetorian guard. And perhaps there had been no other way to do it. The Lord in His wisdom provided the very opportunity that man could not—He made the whole praetorian guard captive to Paul so he could evangelize them.

> What did those soldiers see? Paul's godly character, graciousness, patience, love, wisdom, and conviction. As a result many of the guard may have become a second line of local evangelists, telling all they knew about this unique man who was a prisoner because he preached about Christ. It soon became well known that Paul was in chains because of his zeal to preach Christ. As the praetorian guard was converted, salvation spread beyond them to "those of Caesar's household" (Phil. 4:22).

In the King James Version Philippians 1:13 reads, "My bonds in Christ are manifest in *all the palace*" (emphasis added). The Greek word *praitōrion* could refer either to a building (such as a commander's headquarters, a general's residence, a wealthy person's house, or the emperor's palace) or the group of men who made up the Roman imperial guard. Since Paul was not in the palace but in a private house, most commentators think *praitōrion* refers to the imperial guards who were in charge of guarding Paul. They were associated with the emperor's palace because they guarded the emperor and furthered his interests.

Paul's impact was derived from more than just his ability to articulate the gospel and his godly life-style. The intense affliction Paul endured must have lent tremendous credence to his message and actions. The guards all knew how he suffered and that his life was on the line. That must have produced a certain awe in them toward Paul. So Caesar's household began to fill up with saints.

Commentator F. B. Meyer wrote, "At times the hired room would be thronged with people, to whom the Apostle spoke words of life; and after they withdrew the sentry would sit beside him, filled with many questionings as to the meaning of the words which this strange prisoner spoke. At other times, when all had gone, and especially at night . . . soldier and Apostle would be left to talk, and in those dark, lonely hours the Apostle would tell soldier after soldier the story of his own proud career in early life, of his opposition to Christ, and his ultimate conversion, and would make it clear that he was there as a prisoner, not for any crime, not because he had raised rebellion or revolt, but because he believed that He whom the Roman soldiers had crucified, under Pilate, was the Son of God and the Saviour of men. . . .

"If there had been the least divergence, day or night, from the high standard which he upheld, his soldier-companion would have caught at it and passed it on to others. The fact that so many became earnest Christians, and that the Word of Jesus was known far and wide throughout the praetorian guard, indicates how absolutely consistent the Apostle's life was" (*The Epistle to the Philippians* [Grand Rapids: Baker, 1952], pp. 36-37).

2. Paul's ministry to the city

Beyond the praetorian guard, Paul's confinement gained him attention throughout the city. Acts 28 tells us that many Jewish people visited Paul, and some believed (vv. 23-24). For the two years of his confinement Paul "was welcoming all who came to him, preaching the kingdom of God, and teaching concerning the Lord Jesus Christ with all openness, unhindered" (vv. 30-31).

Paul became headline news—he became known "to everyone else" (Phil. 1:13). Rome wasn't so big that word of Paul and his message couldn't spread. In our own country, if an entire branch of government were significantly impacted by the gospel, the whole country would know. "Everyone else" embraces the whole of Rome.

You may find yourself thinking, *I can't go and preach the gospel. I can't be an evangelist, a missionary, a pastor, or a Bible teacher. I'm stuck with my job.* But the lesson here is that it doesn't matter whether you're chained to a desk, an assembly line, a classroom, a car, or a sales position—they all provide opportunities for you to further the gospel. Whatever you're chained to, you must live in a way that renders the gospel believable. The worse your confinement, the greater the opportunity for a godly life to shine. People often tell me how hard it is to witness where they work. However, my theory is that it is generally harder to witness under ideal conditions than in difficult situations. That's because in difficult situations the reality of a transformed life is more apparent and more clearly attractive.

B. The Advance of Christ's Cause Inside the Church (v. 14)

"Most of the brethren, trusting in the Lord because of my imprisonment, have far more courage to speak the word of God without fear."

Paul's imprisonment also had an impact within the church at Rome. The implication of verse 14 is that before Paul's imprisonment, the church in Rome lacked courage. Paul's witness from his place of confinement was having a marvelous effect on the church's boldness.

The church's lack of boldness is understandable. The Jewish leaders in Rome had told Paul that Christianity was "spoken against everywhere" (Acts 28:22). Paul himself was a living example of the current hostility to the gospel. Doubtless many in leadership were saying, "We don't want to end up in jail! If we want to keep our freedom we'd better not say much."

They may also have feared that their imprisonment would halt the progress of the gospel. We often see that attitude among Christian leadership in our own country. In our desperation to maintain our religious freedoms, we forget that in Communist China the church has flourished better under restrictions than the church in the United States has in our democratic society. God overrules obstacles and purifies His church through adversity.

When the church in Rome saw that God provided for Paul and enabled him to have an incredible opportunity for outreach, "most of the brethren"—the majority—confidently proclaimed the gospel. They realized that since God could minister through Paul in his condition, He could minister through them as well. As Paul's strength became theirs, the leadership in Rome began "to speak the word of God without fear" (v. 14).

Paul's joy was strictly related to the advance of the gospel. His chains benefited not only the church, but they had also become an effective line of communication to the elite soldiers of the Roman empire, who were in a position to carry the gospel to the ends of the earth.

Conclusion

Does your joy ebb and flow according to the tide of earthly benefits? Do pleasure, possessions, prominence, prestige, reputation, comfort, and fulfillment of your own ambitions propel your joy? If they do, your joy will ebb and flow according to the shifting tides of life. But if your joy is tied to the progress of the gospel, it will never diminish. Fix your heart on the progress of the gospel, and your joy will be as constant as the extension of God's kingdom.

Focusing on the Facts

1. What is the theme of Philippians 1:12-26 (see p. 7)?
2. What is one measure of a believer's spiritual maturity (see p. 7)?
3. Nothing short of _____ should steal our joy (see p. 8).
4. When we yield to the working of God's Spirit in our lives, our _____ will not _____ us (see p. 8).
5. How were Paul's circumstances in Rome different from what he had originally planned (see p. 8)?
6. Explain how Paul ended up in Rome (see p. 9).
7. Explain the unusual circumstances of Paul's imprisonment (see pp. 9-10).
8. How did the Philippian church react to Paul's imprisonment (see pp. 10-11)?
9. What was Paul's joy centered on (see p. 11)?
10. What is significant about the phrase "I want you to know" in Philippians 1:12 (see p. 12)?
11. What does the term "brethren" express about Paul's relationship with the Philippian church (see p. 12)?
12. True or false: In verse 12 Paul is emphasizing that things had turned out exactly as one might expect (see p. 12).
13. Explain the meaning of the Greek word *prokopē* and give an illustration of it (see p. 13).
14. What is the probable meaning of the Greek word *praitōrion* in Philippians 1:13? Explain (see p. 15).
15. What were the results of Paul's ministry in the city of Rome (Phil. 1:13; 4:22; see p. 16)?
16. Why is it generally harder to witness under ideal conditions than in more difficult situations (see p. 16)?
17. What marvelous effect did Paul's ministry have on the church in Rome (Phil. 1:14; see p. 17)?

Pondering the Principles

1. In a world wracked with pain, violence, and heartache, a person who radiates joy is a rare commodity. Yet joy is to be the distinctive of every Christian, making him or her winsome to those seeking spiritual answers in an unbelieving world. Puritan Thomas Watson wrote, "Spiritual joy is a sweet and delightful passion, arising from the apprehension and feeling of [God's goodness and favor], whereby the soul is supported under present troubles, and fenced against future fear" (*A Body of Divinity* [Edinburgh: Banner of Truth, 1965], p. 267). Who does not desire such joy? Is your life characterized by a joy that makes unbelievers wonder what you have that they don't?

2. To have joy in the midst of trials requires a mind fixed on something trials cannot touch. Thomas Manton said, "If a man would lead a happy life, let him but seek a sure object for his trust, and he shall be safe: 'He shall not be afraid of evil tidings: his heart is fixed, trusting the Lord' [Ps. 112:7]. He hath laid up his confidence in God, therefore his heart is kept in an equal poise" (cited in *The Golden Treasury of Puritan Quotations*, I.D.E. Thomas, ed. [Edinburgh: Banner of Truth, 1977], p. 160). What determines the joy in your life—your shifting circumstances or the Lord Jesus Christ, the rock of salvation (cf. Matt. 7:24-27)?

Philippians 1:15-18 Tape GC 50-8

2
Joy in Spite of Detractors

Outline

Introduction
A. Trust: The Basis of the Ministry
B. Trust in God: The Solace of the Minister

Review
I. Joy in Spite of Trouble (vv. 12-14)

Lesson
II. Joy in Spite of Detractors (vv. 15-18)
    A. Paul's Situation (vv. 15-17)
        1. The attitude of Paul's detractors
            a) They were jealous
            b) They were contentious
            c) They made false accusations against Paul
                (1) Some said he was being chastened
                (2) Some said he lacked God's power
                (3) Some said he was being replaced
                (4) Some said he was playing politics
        2. The attitude of Paul's supporters
        3. The motives of Paul's supporters
            a) Their love for Paul
            b) Their understanding of his ministry
        4. The motives of Paul's detractors
            a) Their selfish ambitions
            b) Their desire to hurt Paul
    B. Paul's Response (v. 18)

Conclusion

Introduction

When I have the opportunity to speak to pastors and church leaders I am often asked, "What has been the most discouraging thing in your ministry?" As far as I can remember, my answer has remained consistent over the years.

There are two issues that deeply distress me. One is seeing those who ought to be the most mature in the faith—the ones who know the Word of God well, have experienced the blessings of spiritual growth and fellowship, and have seen God's power demonstrated time and again—turn their backs on the faith and embrace sin. That's much more discouraging than when a new, untrained Christian falls into sin through ignorance.

The other thing that most distresses me is being falsely accused by fellow preachers of the gospel. Some men seem to desire to discredit the ministry of others. As a result they falsely accuse other ministers, not because they have valid reasons, but simply to discredit them.

Paul is dealing with that second situation in Philippians 1:15-18: "Some, to be sure, are preaching Christ even from envy and strife, but some also from good will; the latter do it out of love, knowing that I am appointed for the defense of the gospel; the former proclaim Christ out of selfish ambition, rather than from pure motives, thinking to cause me distress in my imprisonment. What then? Only that in every way, whether in pretense or in truth, Christ is proclaimed; and in this I rejoice, yes, and I will rejoice."

    A. Trust: The Basis of the Ministry

> The pain runs deep when preachers of the gospel slander, malign, misrepresent, criticize, accuse, oppose, or belittle one's ministry. That's because trust is an essential aspect of any ministry. A reputation of faithfulness to God's Word is so important that men who go into the ministry need to spend their early years concentrating on laying a foundation of integrity and credibility. That requires a firm commitment to diligent study of God's Word so that when people check the Word for themselves (as the noble Bereans did; Acts 17:10-11) they can see that what you've said is true. It also means a minister's life must conform to

God's Word so that people see a godly life underpinning and confirming his teaching. People will believe and trust that kind of minister.

A minister who cannot be trusted is like a doctor whose patients consistently don't make it through surgery. The doctor wants people to have confidence in him, but as word gets around, patients will stop coming to see him. Similarly, people won't go to a mechanic if they get their car back in worse shape than when they took it in.

Ministry is based on trust. Ministers speak and teach, and congregations either believe or disbelieve what is said. When a minister has spent years establishing a credible ministry, it hurts when that foundation is attacked and slandered.

B. Trust in God: The Solace of the Minister

Jesus was falsely accused. The population of Jerusalem turned on Him and killed Him, yet He had not done, said, or even thought anything wrong. When they determined to kill Him, He did not strike back but committed Himself to God. That's also the example Paul gave us.

Puritan Thomas Manton said, "God is the most powerful asserter of our innocency; He has the hearts and tongues of men in His own hands, and can either prevent the slanderer from uttering reproach, or the hearer from the entertainment of the reproach. He that hath such power over the consciences of men can clear up our innocency; therefore it is best to deal with God about it; and prayer many times proves a better vindication than [self-defense]" (cited in *The Golden Treasury of Puritan Quotations*, ed. I.D.E. Thomas [Edinburgh: Banner of Truth Trust, 1977], p. 284).

In the midst of false accusations Paul said, "I rejoice, yes, and I will rejoice" (Phil. 1:18). Those accusations were discouraging, distressing, disheartening, and discomforting. Doubtless they produced pain and disruption in the Body of Christ. Like the factionalists at Corinth, some in Rome were pro-Paul and some were anti-Paul. Yet despite the distress such circumstances invariably cause, Paul found his solace in God and retained his joy.

Charles Simeon wrote, "Let a pious minister arise in the Established Church, and what labours [jealous men will use] to draw away his people: preachings, prayer-meetings, societies, will all be formed for this very end; and persons of popular talent will be brought from a distance to further the base design" (*Expository Outlines on the Whole Bible*, vol. 18 [Grand Rapids: Zondervan, 1955], pp. 19-20). The godly should expect that their service to God will be attacked. But that shouldn't affect our joy, as we see from Paul's example.

Review

I. JOY IN SPITE OF TROUBLE (vv. 12-14; see pp. 11-18)

Lesson

II. JOY IN SPITE OF DETRACTORS (vv. 15-18)

  A. Paul's Situation (vv. 15-17)

"Some, to be sure, are preaching Christ even from envy and strife, but some also from good will; the latter do it out of love, knowing that I am appointed for the defense of the gospel; the former proclaim Christ out of selfish ambition, rather than from pure motives, thinking to cause me distress in my imprisonment."

There were two kinds of men emboldened by Paul's imprisonment in Rome (Phil. 1:14): his supporters and his detractors.

    1. The attitude of Paul's detractors

A detractor is someone who attempts to belittle, devalue, and tear down the reputation of another. It's hard to imagine a faithful man like Paul having to deal with such people, but he did. He was a holy, godly, powerful, successful, and blessed man—just the kind who is threatening to those with big egos and impure motives.

Paul's detractors preached the gospel, but their purpose in doing so was to discredit, defame, accuse, criticize, and dishonor Paul. That's what made their blood flow.

The "some" referred to in verse 15 reflects back to verse 14—"the brethren." Paul adds the phrase "to be sure" to emphasize that the detractors he referred to did indeed preach the gospel. Those men weren't heretics. They weren't Judaizers, gnostics, idol worshipers, or devotees of Greek mythology. They "preached Christ" —the entirety of gospel truth (vv. 15, 17-18). They weren't proclaiming another gospel (Gal. 1:6) or another Jesus (2 Cor. 11:4). It wasn't Paul's theology that bothered his detractors—it was his person.

a) They were jealous

> Paul said their reasons for preaching were "envy and strife" (Phil. 1:15). Paul's detractors were jealous of his giftedness and success. They may also have been jealous that Paul had personally encountered the resurrected, exalted Lord. Paul was a menace to the prominence of his detractors so they tried to displace him from his seat of authority.

b) They were contentious

> The Greek word translated "strife" refers to contention, conflict, and rivalry. Their jealousy pitted them against him, and conflict resulted. That kind of contention is rampant in the church today. Because people are jealous, they focus their whole lives on trying to discredit people who occupy places of blessing, such as evangelists, writers, pastors, teachers, and leaders of various ministries. Like Paul's detractors, they compete with others by using slander, accusation, and criticism—anything to tear another down.

Paul was not writing to gain sympathy but to inform the Philippians how he was doing. His inspired writings show that the Lord takes note not only of what we preach but of why we preach it. The Lord is as concerned about what is in our hearts as what is on our tongues. Jealousy among leaders in today's church is as much a problem as it was in Paul's day.

c) They made false accusations against Paul

Paul didn't specify how his detractors expressed their contention and strife, but it's not difficult to imagine their false accusations against him.

(1) Some said he was being chastened

They may have speculated about some secret sin in Paul's life. They could have pointed to his dramatic change in circumstances—once he had been traveling freely with God's obvious blessing, but now he was in chains. Perhaps they said, "Paul's obviously outside of God's blessing—he must have sinned. If we knew the truth about Paul, we'd know what's in his life that isn't right. God must be chastening him."

That's how legalists operate—they think they can read everyone's mind and know everyone's secrets. If the detractors could have uncovered some sin in Paul's life, they would have.

(2) Some said he lacked God's power

Some may have said, "The reason Paul is in prison is he hasn't learned to tap the resources of God's power like we have." That's the theology of the modern "name it and claim it" movement. They may have thought Paul an example of spiritual impotence, assuming that if he had divine power he would have broken his chains and walked away.

(3) Some said he was being replaced

Still others may have said, "The Lord put Paul in prison and left us free because Paul is old-time, and we're his replacements. It's time for fresh blood in the ministry."

(4) Some said he was playing politics

> There may even have been those who said, "If Paul were truly a godly man he'd have been martyred long ago. The government has him in chains, but instead of being bold and dying for Christ, he's playing politics and trying to get released. He'll probably work some secret deal and get off."

It is sad to think of so dear a saint as Paul going through such pain—eventually to the point of reporting, "At my first defense [the first trial in Rome] no one supported me, but all deserted me" (2 Tim. 4:16). He wrote to Timothy, "All who are in Asia turned away from me" (2 Tim. 1:15). When Paul wrote to the Philippians he was so bereft of friends that he said of Timothy, "I have no one else of kindred spirit" (Phil. 2:20). Paul may have wondered, *Is this what I get in return for all I've done for the church—a bunch of spineless people who won't come to my defense but attack me instead to exalt their own egos?*

2. The attitude of Paul's supporters

On the other hand, Paul wrote that "some also [were preaching Christ] from good will" (v. 15). The Greek word translated "good will" (*eudokian*) denotes satisfaction and contentedness. Paul's supporters were content with what God was doing in their own lives and in Paul's life. They were sympathetic toward Paul and grateful for his ministry. There are also people like that in the church today—what a blessing, encouragement, and source of joy they are! I thank God for filling my life with supporters.

3. The motives of Paul's supporters

   a) Their love for Paul

   Those who supported Paul did so "out of love" (v. 16). Those who preached Christ out of envy and strife certainly weren't characterized by love. An essential element of effective ministry is love. Paul affirmed that truth in 1 Corinthians 13: "If I speak with the tongues of men and of angels, but do not have love, I have become a noisy gong or a clanging cymbal. And if I have the gift of prophecy, and know all mysteries and all knowledge; and if I have all faith, so as to remove mountains, but do not have love, I am nothing" (vv. 1-2). Even though Paul had detractors, there were those who had a deep affection for him and cared about him.

b) Their understanding of his ministry

Paul's supporters knew he was "appointed for the defense of the gospel" (v. 16). They understood the strategic nature of Paul's ministry and knew he was in prison because he was destined—"appointed"—to be there. The Greek word translated "appointed" (*keimai*) was used to describe a soldier's being placed on duty. God put Paul on duty to defend the gospel.

The Greek word translated "defense" is *apologia*, from which we derive the English word *apologetic*. Apologetics is the branch of theology devoted to the defense of the divine origin and authority of Christianity. Paul was a defender of the gospel and had been placed by God in a strategic position to make his stand: before the imperial government in Rome. Paul had already made his defense by the time he wrote to the Philippians (v. 7). He was now awaiting his sentence and may have had that first hearing in mind when he wrote, "I am appointed for the defense of the gospel" (v. 16).

4. The motives of Paul's detractors

a) Their selfish ambitions

In verse 17 Paul explains the motives of his detractors: "The former [the detractors] proclaim Christ out of selfish ambition." In contrast to the love that characterized Paul's supporters, his detractors were motivated by selfish ambition—the most wicked of all motives. They were far removed from the principles of Philippians 2:3: "Do nothing from selfishness or empty conceit, but with humility of mind let each of you regard one another as more important than himself." The Philippians were not to behave like Paul's detractors in Rome.

Although Paul's detractors preached the right message, their motive was wrong. Selfishness appears in many forms. Peter warned against seeking after sordid gain (1 Pet. 5:2) and dominating others (1 Pet. 5:3). The apostle John spoke against seeking to be first (3 John 9). Selfishness can show itself in any of those ways.

The Greek word translated "selfish ambition" (*erithia*) originally meant to work for hire. But it came to be applied in a negative sense to those who sought solely to benefit themselves—to advance themselves by acquiring wealth and prestige. It was often used of those who promote themselves in the course of running for government office. It was also used of the ruthlessly ambitious—those who sought to elevate themselves at all costs. Paul's imprisonment provided the perfect opportunity for such people to enhance their personal prestige and decrease his.

b) Their desire to hurt Paul

Paul said his detractors were thinking to cause him distress during his imprisonment (v. 17). They weren't concerned with the church, the purity of its doctrine, or its growth. They just wanted to hurt Paul so they could be on top. "Thinking" refers to planning and scheming. They came up with various ways to aggravate Paul's already distressing situation. By attacking his integrity, credibility, faithfulness, and character, they knew they would hurt him—and that, sad to say, was their objective.

"Distress" (Gk., *thlipsis*) means "friction." The malicious behavior of Paul's detractors increased the friction of his chains. Far from exalting Christ, protecting the church, evangelizing the lost, or defending the Word of God, their goal was to irritate Paul.

Remember, Paul wasn't writing to garner sympathy. His words serve as a warning: we ought not to be surprised by similar behavior in the church today. It happened to Paul and can happen to us. Many times the New Testament warns against envy, strife, selfish ambition, and impure motives (cf. Rom. 1:29; 2 Cor. 12:20; Gal. 5:20-21; 1 Tim. 6:4). Those warnings are as relevant now as they were then.

B. Paul's Response (v. 18)

"What then? Only that in every way, whether in pretense or in truth, Christ is proclaimed; and in this I rejoice, yes, and I will rejoice."

Paul didn't allow his circumstances to steal his joy. That's the important lesson we should learn. What mattered most to Paul was that the truth of Christ was proclaimed.

The Greek word translated "proclaimed" (*katangelloti*) means "to proclaim with authority." Regardless of the personal cost, Paul was determined that Christ be proclaimed with authority. He could rejoice even if what motivated that proclamation was a desire to attack him (v. 18).

Paul's detractors preached the true gospel, and it had an impact. A selfishly motivated preacher can still be used of God, though not as much as he could be if he had pure motives. God can still use him because the truth is more powerful than its package. After all, the power "lies in the gospel, not the gospeller" (John Eadie, *A Commentary of the Epistle of Paul to the Philippians* [N.Y.: Robert Carter & Bros., 1859], p. 41). Often the listener knows nothing of a preacher's motive and thus concentrates on the message only.

Paul wasn't concerned about himself because he knew he was expendable. He also knew that God defends the innocent and would vindicate him in due time. So he was free to rejoice in the proclamation of the gospel, however base the motives of some preachers. They weren't preaching Buddha or another false god, but Christ. So Paul could earnestly and generously rejoice. He was a man of true spiritual character—unlike many in our day.

Commentator John Daille wrote, "While we detest the abominable profaneness of men who so dreadfully abuse the gospel, let us not cease to rejoice in the good effects which God produces by their hands. Let us hold the thorns of such plants in horror, and gather with thanksgiving the roses which the goodness of God causes to spring from them; and, after the example of the apostle, let us rejoice to see our Christ preached, whatever may be the mind or the hand which presents us His mysteries" (*An Exposition of Philippians* [MacDill AFB, Florida: Tyndale Bible Society, n.d.], p. 37). That's the attitude we're to have.

Conclusion

Paul lived only to see the gospel proclaimed—he didn't care who received the credit. That should be the attitude of every pastor, teacher, elder, deacon, leader, and layperson in the church. In all that he suffered Paul didn't quit, lash out, break down, or lose his joy. That's because the cause of Christ was being furthered and His name proclaimed. It was all Paul cared about. That's an attitude the grace of Christ instills in all who would be godly. Trials and slander are unendurable if handled in the flesh, but those in the Spirit need never lose their joy because of them.

Focusing on the Facts

1. _____ is an essential aspect of any ministry (see p. 22).
2. Despite the distress caused by his circumstances, Paul found solace. What did he find it in? What did that allow him to do (see p. 23)?
3. What did Charles Simeon say would happen if "a pious minister" arose in an established church (see p. 24)?
4. What two kinds of men were emboldened by Paul's presence in Rome (see p. 24)?
5. What does a detractor do? What specifically did Paul's detractors do (see p. 24)?
6. Did Paul's detractors preach a gospel different from Paul's? Explain (see p. 25).
7. Why were Paul's detractors jealous of Paul (see p. 25)?

8. _____ among leaders in today's church is as much a problem as it was in Paul's day (see p. 26).
9. What are four accusations Paul's detractors might have fabricated to discredit him (see pp. 26-27)?
10. What does the Greek word translated "good will" (*eudokian*) denote (see p. 27)?
11. What motives explain the attitude of Paul's supporters (see pp. 27-28)?
12. What motives explain the attitude of Paul's detractors (see pp. 28-30)?
13. What was the only thing that mattered to Paul (see p. 30)?
14. How can God use the gospel message of a selfishly motivated preacher (see p. 30)?
15. Why didn't Paul quit, lash out, break down, or lose his joy (see p. 31)?

Pondering the Principles

1. How was Paul able to maintain his joy and be patient with those who ought to have been treating him as a brother but were in fact treating him like an enemy? Jerry Bridges writes, "One of the thoughts that most disturbs a suffering Christian who has not learned patience is [the] issue of justice. He is concerned that his tormentor will escape justice, that he will not receive the punishment he deserves. The patient Christian who suffers leaves this issue in the hands of God. He is confident that God will render justice. . . . Instead of hoping and waiting for an opportunity for revenge, he prays for God's forgiveness of his tormentors, just as Jesus and the martyr Stephen prayed for their executioners" (*The Practice of Godliness* [Colorado Springs, Co.: Navpress, 1983], pp. 205-6). Does that kind of forbearance toward others and trust in God characterize your response toward those in the church who treat you badly?

2. Paul's attitude toward his persecutors indicates that he was more concerned with the salvation of the lost than with personal vindication. That's precisely the attitude we find in Paul's description of our Lord in Philippians 2:5-8: He gave up His divine reputation and privileges that men and women might be delivered from the power of sin. Puritan Thomas Watson pointed out that Christ "came not in the majesty of a king, attended

with his [bodyguards], but he came poor; not like the heir of heaven, but like one of inferior descent. The place he was born in was poor; not the royal city Jerusalem, but Bethlehem, a poor obscure place. He was born in an inn, and a manger was his cradle, the cobwebs his curtains, the beasts his companions; he descended of poor parents" (*Body of Divinity* [Edinburgh: Banner of Truth Trust, 1965 reprint], p. 196). Reflect the attitude of Christ in your life by putting sinners and their salvation uppermost in your priorities.

Philippians 1:19-21 — Tape GC 50-9

3
Joy in Spite of Death

Outline

Introduction

Review
I. Joy in Spite of Trouble (vv. 12-14)
II. Joy in Spite of Detractors (vv. 15-18)

Lesson
III. Joy in Spite of Death (vv. 19-21)
    A. Paul's Confidence (vv. 19-20)
        1. He was confident of being delivered by God
            a) God's promise
            b) Paul's deliverance
            c) Paul's conviction
        2. He was confident in the prayers of the saints
        3. He was confident in the provision of the Spirit
        4. He was confident in the promise of heaven
        5. He was confident in the plan of God
    B. Paul's Commitment (v. 21)
        1. In life
        2. In death

Conclusion

Introduction

The New Testament passages that deal with Paul's life show that events went badly for him. Acts 9 records Paul's salvation, but by the end of the chapter people were already plotting to kill him, and he was forced to flee to save his life. He was initially rejected by the church at Jerusalem (Acts 9:26). On his first missionary journey, he was publicly contradicted and accused of blasphemy. Mobs were stirred up against him. In Lystra Paul was stoned and left for dead.

Paul himself said, "[I am] in far more labors, in far more imprisonments, beaten times without number, often in danger of death. Five times I received from the Jews thirty-nine lashes. Three times I was beaten with rods, once I was stoned, three times I was shipwrecked, a night and a day I have spent in the deep. I have been on frequent journeys, in dangers from rivers, dangers from robbers, dangers from my countrymen, dangers from the Gentiles, dangers in the city, dangers in the wilderness, dangers on the sea, dangers among false brethren; I have been in labor and hardship, through many sleepless nights, in hunger and thirst, often without food, in cold and exposure. Apart from such external things, there is the daily pressure upon me of concern for all the churches" (2 Cor. 11:23-28). He was forsaken by unfaithful friends (2 Tim. 1:15). Of Timothy he wrote, "I have no one else of kindred spirit" (Phil. 2:20).

Many of the churches into which Paul poured his time and energy fell into gross sin and erroneous theology. He had continual sorrow for the lost condition of his own people (Rom. 9:1-3). Many individuals he nurtured had defected from the faith or had left him to serve elsewhere (cf. 2 Tim. 4:10). He was imprisoned at least five times—in Jerusalem, Caesarea, Philippi, and twice in Rome. One wonders if when Paul entered a city he checked out the local jail to see where he'd be spending the night!

Yet Paul never lost his joy. In the midst of trials he was "sorrowful yet always rejoicing" (2 Cor. 6:10). Bad circumstances increase the joy of those who respond biblically because they lead to a deeper trust in God. Joy derived from circumstances is fleeting, but joy derived from a relationship with Christ is lasting.

Review

I. JOY IN SPITE OF TROUBLE (vv. 12-14; pp. 11-18)

II. JOY IN SPITE OF DETRACTORS (vv. 15-18; pp. 24-31)

Lesson

III. JOY IN SPITE OF DEATH (vv. 19-21)

> "I know that this shall turn out for my deliverance through your prayers and the provision of the Spirit of Jesus Christ, according to my earnest expectation and hope, that I shall not be put to shame in anything, but that with all boldness, Christ shall even now, as always, be exalted in my body, whether by life or by death. For to me, to live is Christ, and to die is gain."

Paul remained joyful as long as his Lord was glorified, even though he was threatened with death. All that mattered to him was that the gospel was advanced, Christ was preached, and the Lord was magnified. The source of his joy was entirely related to the kingdom of God.

Few in today's church are committed to Jesus Christ as the apostle Paul was. Paul exemplifies what Christ was talking about when He said, "If anyone wishes to come after Me, let him deny himself, and take up his cross daily, and follow Me" (Luke 9:23; cf. 14:27). Paul was so given over to our Lord that he didn't care whether he lived or died. That's an attitude practically unheard of in our materialistic, self-centered, selfish day. Most people today live for anything *except* what Paul was focused on.

A. Paul's Confidence (vv. 19-20)

> "I know that this shall turn out for my deliverance through your prayers and the provision of the Spirit of Jesus Christ, according to my earnest expectation and hope, that I shall not be put to shame in anything, but that with all boldness, Christ shall even now, as always, be exalted in my body, whether by life or by death."

Paul was confident of five things in the face of death.

1. He was confident of being delivered by God

a) God's promise

When Paul said, "I know [Gk., *oida*] that this shall turn out for my deliverance," he was saying he had a settled conviction. He knew his present trials would turn out for his future deliverance, believing that "God causes all things to work together for good to those who love God, to those who are called according to His purpose" (Rom. 8:28).

b) Paul's deliverance

The Greek word translated "deliverance" (*soteria*) is the word for salvation. That's how the King James Version translates it, although *soteria* can also be translated "well-being" or "escape." As a result of those varying possibilities, some say Paul was referring to his ultimate salvation. Others think he was referring to his deliverance from threatened execution. Still others think he was referring to personal vindication—that when his sentence from the emperor was finally rendered he would be vindicated. Some commentators think Paul was referring to eventual release from prison. I think there is a measure of truth in each of those interpretations. The key thought is that Paul knew his current distress was only temporary and that he would be delivered from it.

c) Paul's conviction

Why was Paul convinced of his deliverance? His statement "I know that this shall turn out for my deliverance" is a quote of the Greek version of Job 13:16. Job was a righteous man who suffered greatly, yet he was delivered because God always delivers the righteous. Job said, "Though . . . worms destroy this body, yet in my flesh shall I see God" (Job 19:26; KJV). He knew that either temporally or eternally God would deliver him.

Paul knew the Old Testament and may have identified with Job. He knew he could trust God to deliver him just as God had delivered Job. Like Job, Paul wasn't being chastened by God. He was confident his circumstances would work out for good whether he was released from prison, vindicated at his trial, rescued from execution, or delivered into glory as a martyr.

Paul didn't know he would be released from prison because he said his deliverance would come "by life or death" (v. 20). Like the affirmations found in many of the Psalms (Ps. 22:4-5, 8; 31:1; 33:18-19; 34:7; 41:1), Paul was confident that God would deliver the righteous.

2. He was confident in the prayers of the saints

Paul was confident that he would be delivered through the prayers of the Philippians (v. 19). He believed in the sovereign will and purpose of God, and knew that He would bring His purposes to pass in concert with the prayers of His children. He also knew that "the effectual prayer of a righteous man can accomplish much" (James 5:16). The love and prayers of the saints in Philippi encouraged Paul greatly.

We see Paul's reliance on prayer in other passages of Scripture as well.

a) Romans 15:30—"I urge you, brethren, by our Lord Jesus Christ and by the love of the Spirit, to strive together with me in your prayers to God for me."

b) Ephesians 6:18-19—"With all prayer and petition pray at all times in the Spirit . . . with all perseverance and petition for all the saints, and pray on my behalf, that utterance may be given to me in the opening of my mouth, to make known with boldness the mystery of the gospel for which I am an ambassador in chains."

c) 1 Thessalonians 5:25—"Brethren, pray for us."

3. He was confident in the provision of the Spirit

Paul was also confident in "the provision of the Spirit of Jesus Christ" (v. 19). The Word, prayer, and the Spirit all work together for the benefit of God's servants.

The Greek word translated "provision" (*epichorēgia*) means "help," "bountiful supply," or "full resources." Paul was speaking of the resources of the Spirit. He grants all that is necessary to sustain the righteous.

The Holy Spirit is called "the Spirit of Christ" and "the Spirit of God" (Rom. 8:9). He can be called by either title because He is part of the Trinity and proceeds from the Father in the name of Christ (cf. John 14:26). Paul knew the Holy Spirit as his indwelling teacher, interceder, guide, source of power, and all-sufficient provider. That's what the Spirit is for all believers.

a) Zechariah 4:6—God provides for believers "not by might nor by power, but by [God's] Spirit."

b) John 14:16—Jesus was referring to the coming of the Holy Spirit when He said, "I will ask the Father, and He will give you another Helper, that He may be with you forever."

c) John 16:13—Jesus promised, "When He, the Spirit of truth, comes, He will guide you into all the truth; for He will not speak on His own initiative, but whatever He hears, He will speak; and He will disclose to you what is to come."

d) Acts 1:8—Jesus said to the apostles, "You shall receive power when the Holy Spirit has come upon you."

e) Romans 8:26—Paul's confidence that all things work together for good (v. 28) was based on the provision of the Spirit, who "helps our weakness; for we do not know how to pray as we should, but the Spirit Himself intercedes for us with groanings too deep for words."

f) Galatians 5:22—"The fruit of the Spirit is love, joy, peace, patience, kindness, goodness, faithfulness, gentleness, self-control"—all that a believer needs.

g) Ephesians 3:20—God "is able to do exceeding abundantly beyond all that we ask or think, according to the power that works in us."

Knowing the Spirit's provision, Paul could face death with tremendous confidence.

4. He was confident in the promise of heaven

In Philippians 1:20 Paul says, "According to my earnest expectation and hope, [I know] that I shall not be put to shame in anything, but that with all boldness, Christ shall even now, as always, be exalted in my body." He was surely confident of Christ's promise in Matthew 10:32: "Everyone . . . who shall confess Me before men, I will also confess him before My Father who is in heaven." He also had the assurance of this promise at the time of his conversion: "the God of our fathers has appointed you [Paul] to know His will, and to see the Righteous One, and to bear an utterance from His mouth. For you will be a witness for Him to all men of what you have seen and heard" (Acts 22:14-15; cf. Acts 9:15).

The extent of Paul's confidence may be seen by his use of the Greek word *apokaradokia*, translated "earnest expectation." It's "a picturesque word, denoting a state of keen anticipation of the future, the craning of the neck to catch a glimpse of what lies ahead" (Ralph P. Martin, *New Century Bible: Philippians* [Greenwood, S.C.: Attic Press, 1976], pp. 75-76). Paul rejoiced that he would never be put to shame before the world, the court of Caesar, or God Himself because he knew God would be glorified in his life.

The Old Testament affirms that the righteous will never be put to shame, whereas the unrighteous will (cf. Pss. 25:2-3; 35:25-27; 40:15-16; 69:6-7; 119:80; Isa. 1:27-29; 45:14-17; 49:23; 50:7; Jer. 12:13; and Zeph. 3:11). To be put to shame means to be disappointed, disillusioned, or disgraced. Paul knew that would never happen to him because of God's promise to the righteous. He may have had Isaiah 49:23 in mind: "Those who hope in me will not be disappointed" (NIV*). In fact he quoted it in Romans 9:33.

5. He was confident in the plan of God

Paul didn't know God's specific plan for his life, but he was confident in it, whether it meant life or death (v. 20). In verses 23-24 he says, "I am hard-pressed from both directions, having the desire to depart and be with Christ, for that is very much better, yet to remain in the flesh is more necessary for your sake." Paul preferred the joy of being in Christ's presence in heaven, but apparently he thought the Lord would let him live because he knew the Philippians needed him.

Paul rejoiced because he knew that by either his life or death Christ would be exalted. If he lived he would be free to preach and build the church. If he died he would be executed for Christ's sake and his unwavering faith would serve as a trophy of Christ's grace. For Paul the issue was not his troubles, detractors, or even the possibility of his death, but whether the gospel was advancing and the Lord was being magnified.

B. Paul's Commitment (v. 21)

"To me, to live is Christ, and to die is gain."

1. In life

That reflects what Paul saw as the *summum bonum* of his life. Christ was Paul's raison d'être—his reason for being. He wasn't merely saying that Christ was the source of his life, that Christ lived in him, or that Christ wanted Paul to submit to Him. Though all those statements are true in themselves, they are only parts of this great truth: life in its sum is Christ.

New International Version.

2. In death

Since Christ was Paul's whole life, dying could only be gain since it would relieve him of the burdens of his present life and free him to focus completely on glorifying his Lord. That's what he lived for anyway—Paul truly had a one-track mind!

In Acts 20:23-24 Paul says to the Ephesian elders, "The Holy Spirit witnesseth in every city, saying that bonds and afflictions await me. But none of these things move me, neither count I my life dear unto myself, so that I might finish my course with joy, and the ministry, which I have received of the Lord Jesus, to testify the gospel of grace of God" (KJV). He was warned that he would be imprisoned and in chains, but his response was, "I am ready not only to be bound, but even to die . . . for the name of the Lord Jesus" (Acts 21:13). That's to be the attitude of every Christian.

In William Shakespeare's play *Hamlet* the young prince wonders whether to relieve the sorrows of life by suicide, musing, "To be, or not to be, that is the question" (act 3, scene 1, line 61). To Paul the issue was, "To live is Christ, and to die is gain" (Phil. 1:21).

Conclusion

Personalize Paul's message for a moment. Read verse 21 as, "For me, to live is _____ , and to die is _____ ." Then fill in the blanks. If you put "wealth" in the first blank, dying brings not gain but loss. The same is true if you selected prestige, fame, power, or possessions, because none of those things remains after death: prestige is lost, fame is forgotten, power is useless, and possessions are taken by others. For verse 21 to make sense as Paul wrote it, only Christ can fill the first blank. Otherwise death is inevitably a loss.

Many who read this will say, "I put Christ in my blank." But if they think about it carefully, they will realize that what they really meant was Christ plus wealth, Christ plus power, or Christ plus possessions. Christ can't share the first blank with anything else. Those who truly live for Christ have no fear of death and make the best use of life: in both they glorify Christ. That was Paul's attitude, and it should be ours as well.

Focusing on the Facts

1. How do bad circumstances provide the opportunity to increase our joy (see p. 36)?
2. What really mattered to Paul when he was faced with death (see p. 37)?
3. How does the attitude of Paul compare with the attitude of most people in our own day (see p. 37)?
4. What does Paul's use of the Greek word *oida* in Philippians 1:19 imply (see p. 38)?
5. What are the varying interpretations of the Greek word translated "deliverance" (*soteria*) (see p. 38)?
6. Why was Paul convinced that he would be delivered (see pp. 38-39)?
7. Why did Paul take comfort in the prayers of the Philippians (see p. 39)?
8. What passages of Scripture show the confidence of Paul in prayer (see p. 39)?
9. What did Paul probably mean when he spoke of "the provision of the Spirit" (Phil. 1:19; see p. 40)?
10. Explain Paul's "earnest expectation and hope" (Phil. 1:20; see pp. 41-42).
11. What does the Old Testament affirm about the righteous and the unrighteous regarding shame (see pp. 41-42)?
12. If Paul could have chosen life or death, which would he have preferred? Why (see p. 42)?
13. What was the *summum bonum* of Paul's life (see p. 42)?
14. According to the example of Paul, what ought to be the attitude of every Christian (see pp. 43-44)?

Pondering the Principles

1. Our world knows little of what it means to be happy in the midst of a trial. Happiness is understood to be a function of mood, possessions, or place—not a confidence that rests com-

pletely outside of this world. American pastor A. W. Tozer wrote, "In this day of universal apprehension when men's hearts are failing them for fear of those things that are coming upon the earth, we Christians are strategically placed to display a happiness that is not of this world and to exhibit a tranquillity that will be a little bit of heaven here below" (*Signposts: A Collection of Sayings from A. W. Tozer*, Harry Verploegh, ed. [Wheaton, Ill.: Victor, 1988], p. 96). Do those who know you see in your life a happiness based in heaven or on earth?

2. We often forget that the Christian life here on earth is by necessity a battle. Certainly Paul knew that reality, yet he also knew the battle was worth the cost. J. C. Ryle said, "The Christian's fight is good, because it ends in a glorious reward for all who fight it. Who can tell the wages that Christ will pay to all His faithful people? Who can estimate the good things that our divine Captain has laid up for those who confess Him before men? . . . The bravest generals must go down one day before the king of terrors. Better, far better, is the position of him who fights under Christ's banner, against sin, the world and the devil. He may get little praise of man while he lives, and go down to the grave with little honour, but he shall have that which is far better, because [it is] far more enduring" (*Holiness: Its Nature, Hindrances, Difficulties, and Roots* [Welwyn, Eng.: Evangelical Press, 1979], p. 62). Do not be discouraged if in the midst of your present battle to maintain your Christian testimony, you see little reward. You have Christ's promise that "everyone who shall confess Me before men, I will also confess him before My Father who is in heaven" (Matt. 10:32-33).

Philippians 1:22-26   Tape GC 50-10

4
Joy in Spite of the Flesh

Outline

Introduction

Review
I. Joy in Spite of Trouble (vv. 12-14)
II. Joy in Spite of Detractors (vv. 15-18)
III. Joy in Spite of Death (vv. 19-21)

Lesson
IV. Joy in Spite of the Flesh (vv. 22-26)
    A. The Meaning of "Flesh" (v. 22*a*)
    B. The Promise of Fruitful Labor (v. 22*b*)
        1. It is hard spiritual work
        2. It requires a strong desire
    C. The Hard Choice (vv. 22*c*-23*a*)
    D. The Desire to Depart (v. 23*b*)
    E. The Need to Remain (vv. 24-26)
        1. Its necessity (vv. 24-25)
        2. Its purpose (v. 26)

Conclusion

Introduction

The book *To the Golden Shore* tells the story of Adoniram Judson, one of the first American missionaries sent overseas (Courtney Anderson [Grand Rapids: Zondervan, 1956]). He was a brave ambassador of Jesus Christ who served his Lord in what was then known as Burma. After fourteen years of enduring wretched imprisonments and life-threatening diseases, all he had to show for his pains were the graves of his wife and all his children. He was alone, yet he was faithful to remain there. He wrote that if he had not felt certain that every trial was ordered by God's infinite love and mercy, he could not have survived his accumulated sufferings.

Judson understood that his trials were a part of the sovereign plan of God. Although he must have longed to be with Christ and enjoy the fellowship of his beloved family, he also longed to meet the needs of the pagan Burmese people. Therefore he prayed God would allow him to live until he had translated the entire Bible into Burmese and had presided over a native church of at least one hundred Christians.

Judson had the spirit of the apostle Paul, who longed to be with Christ but also desired to be useful to the church: "If I am to live on in the flesh, this will mean fruitful labor for me; and I do not know which to choose. But I am hard-pressed from both directions, having the desire to depart and be with Christ, for that is very much better; yet to remain on in the flesh is more necessary for your sake. And convinced of this, I know that I shall remain and continue with you all for your progress and joy in the faith, so that your proud confidence in me may abound in Christ Jesus through my coming to you again" (Phil. 1:22-26).

Review

I. JOY IN SPITE OF TROUBLE (vv. 12-14; pp. 11-18)

II. JOY IN SPITE OF DETRACTORS (vv. 15-18; pp. 24-31)

III. JOY IN SPITE OF DEATH (vv. 19-21; pp. 37-44)

Lesson

IV. JOY IN SPITE OF THE FLESH (vv. 22-26)

As Paul wrote to the Philippian church he was waiting for the Lord to show him whether he would live or die. In verse 21 he mentions that to die and be with Christ is gain, but he was willing to remain in the flesh if it would benefit the church. Those two equal desires ought to characterize every believer.

A. The Meaning of "Flesh" (v. 22*a*)

"If I am to live in the flesh."

This clearly refers to remaining in this world. Romans 8:5 contrasts those who live "according to the flesh" with "those [who live] according to the Spirit." That's a contrast between unrighteousness and righteousness, but "flesh" can also refer to one's existence in the physical world.

1. 2 Corinthians 10:3—"Though we walk in the flesh, we do not war according to the flesh, for the weapons of our warfare are not of the flesh." Here Paul was not speaking of walking in sin (cf. Gal. 5:16-17, 25) but of simply living in the physical world. Although we exist in the physical realm, we do not fight spiritual battles with physical weapons.

2. Galatians 2:20—Paul said, "I have been crucified with Christ; and it is no longer I who live, but Christ lives in me; and the life which I now live in the flesh I live by faith in the Son of God." Paul didn't mean he was living in sin but that he was living the remainder of his life by faith.

3. 1 Peter 4:2—"Live the rest of the time in the flesh no longer for the lusts of men, but for the will of God."

B. The Promise of Fruitful Labor (v. 22*b*)

"This will mean fruitful labor for me."

1. It is hard spiritual work

If Paul lived on in the physical world, he fully expected his life to result in "fruitful labor." He considered being alive in our world to be synonymous with fruitful labor for Christ. That's the idea behind Philippians 1:21: "To me, to live is Christ."

Paul often used the Greek word translated "labor" (*ergon*) to describe his own ministry. He also uses it to describe Epaphroditus's work in Philippians 2:30: "He came close to death for the *work* of Christ" (emphasis added). Used that way *ergon* refers to spiritual work—work for the Lord.

a) Romans 1:13—Paul said to the Romans, "I have planned to come to you . . . that I might obtain some fruit among you." That's a reference to converts.

b) 1 Corinthians 16:15—"The household of Stephanus . . . were the first fruits of Achaia."

c) Galatians 5:22-23—"The fruit of the Spirit is love, joy, peace, patience, kindness, goodness, faithfulness, gentleness, self-control."

d) Philippians 1:11—As Christians we're to be "filled with the fruit of righteousness."

e) Hebrews 13:15—We are to offer a sacrifice of praise to God, "that is, the fruit of lips that give thanks to His name."

Spiritual fruit may be people, deeds, or words—whatever is of eternal value. That kind of fruit comes from honest hard work, which is the natural activity of the godly on earth.

2. It requires a strong desire

Paul had a strong desire to stay and bear fruit. He wanted the Philippians to be confident in Christ and strengthened for evangelism (Phil. 1:26-27). He's reminiscent of the psalmist who said, "O God, Thou hast taught me from my youth; and I still declare Thy wondrous deeds. And even when I am old and gray, O God, do not forsake me, until I declare Thy strength to this generation, Thy power to all who are to come" (Ps. 71:17-18). That elderly man wanted to live long enough to declare God's strength and power to the next generation.

King Hezekiah was about to die an early death, but God was gracious to him and healed him. The king declared, "Sheol cannot thank Thee, death cannot praise Thee; those who go down to the pit cannot hope for Thy faithfulness. It is the living who give thanks to Thee, as I do today; a father tells his sons about Thy faithfulness" (Isa. 38:18-19). Like Paul, Hezekiah desired to communicate the greatness of God to others.

C. The Hard Choice (vv. 22c-23a)

"I do not know which to choose. . . . I am hard-pressed from both directions."

Death would have ushered Paul into the presence of his Lord, yet life provided the opportunity to advance the kingdom. The phrase "I do not know" contains a Greek word Paul often used—*gnōrizō*. Of the twenty-six times it occurs in the New Testament, eighteen of those occurrences are in Paul's writings. It means "to reveal" or "make known." Paul couldn't decide what to choose. He knew it was an issue that was in the Lord's hands, and, given the choice, couldn't choose either heaven or earth for himself.

Choosing Between Heaven and Earth

You may find yourself in the same dilemma Paul faced. Every Christian ought to feel the strain of desiring to be with Christ, yet also longing to build His church. If the Lord said to me, "You have five minutes to choose between being in heaven or on earth," I would have a difficult time making that decision. And I would want to be sure I was basing my choice on the right reasons.

The only legitimate reason that would make that choice difficult is uncertainty as to whether you could glorify Christ more in heaven or on earth. Paul found it an impossible choice. Nevertheless, most people would choose to stay on earth. When asked why they would say, "We're getting a new house," "We're going on a trip," or, "I don't want to leave my kids." For Paul, nothing really mattered except glorifying Christ. When faced with the most basic of life's issues—whether it would be better to live or die—his response was, "I would be thrilled to glorify Christ in heaven or on

> earth. Given the choice, I can't choose." Because glorifying Christ was Paul's motivation, the place where he glorified Christ was not the issue. That ought to be true for every believer.

Because Paul couldn't choose, he wrote, "I am hard-pressed from both directions" (v. 23). "Hard-pressed" (Gk., *sunechō*) speaks of being hemmed in on both sides. It pictures a traveler on a narrow path, a wall of rock on either side. He is unable to turn aside and able only to go straight ahead (William Barclay, *The Letters to the Philippians, Colossians, and Thessalonians*, rev. ed. [Philadelphia: Westminster, 1975], p. 27). Paul felt pressured by both possibilities and didn't know which way God would lead.

Paul had "the desire to depart and be with Christ" (v. 23) yet also "to remain on in the flesh" (v. 24). His two desires were equally strong and equally good—it wasn't a choice between one alternative and something better. His was not the dilemma of David, who was presented with several choices from the Lord, all of which would cause him great distress. Yet in that situation, David discerned that one of the choices was better than the others, saying, "I am in great distress [at the choices presented to me]. Let us . . . fall into the hand of the Lord for His mercies are great, but do not let me fall into the hand of man" (2 Sam. 24:14).

D. The Desire to Depart (v. 23*b*)

"Having the desire to depart and be with Christ, for that is very much better."

The Greek word translated "desire" (*epithumia*) is most often used to describe sinful lust. But occasionally it expresses a strong unfulfilled desire for something right and good. Paul had a compelling but unfulfilled desire to "depart" (Gk., *analusi*). That is the same word used in 2 Timothy 4:6: "I am already being poured out as a drink offering, and the time of my *departure* is at hand" (emphasis added). He expresses the same idea in 2 Corinthians 5:8: "We are of good courage, I say, and prefer . . . to be absent from the body and to be at home with the Lord." Unlike the desire of Greek philosophers for immortality of the soul in a vague sense, Paul's great desire was to be in personal, intimate, complete, unhindered, conscious fellowship with Christ.

Absent from the Body, Present with the Lord

When a believer leaves this world he goes immediately to be in the presence of Christ. There is no "soul sleep" or intermediate waiting place. Nor does the Bible teach that there is any place called purgatory. Paul's desire was "to depart and *be with Christ*" (Phil. 1:23, emphasis added).

- Acts 7:59-60—As Stephen was being stoned to death "he called upon the Lord and said, 'Lord Jesus, receive my spirit!' And falling on his knees, he cried out with a loud voice, 'Lord, do not hold this sin against them!' And having said this, he fell asleep." Stephen's spirit was received into Christ's presence as his body "fell asleep," or died. The biblical writers often described death as falling asleep in light of the resurrection, which is when the body rises again.

- 2 Corinthians 5:6-8—"While we are at home in the body we are absent from the Lord—for we walk by faith, not by sight . . . and prefer rather to be absent from the body and to be at home with the Lord." When we are absent from the body, which sleeps until the resurrection, our spirit is at home with the Lord.

- 1 Thessalonians 5:10—The Lord Jesus Christ "died for us, that whether we are awake or asleep, we may live together with Him." Paul's point is that whether we are physically awake (alive) or physically asleep (dead), as believers we are with Christ. We are in His presence in a spiritual sense now and in a literal sense when our bodies are dead.

There is no time in the life of a believer when he or she will ever be out of the conscious presence of Jesus Christ.

According to Paul, being in Christ's literal presence is "very much better" (Phil. 1:23). More than "better" or "much better," to be with Christ so far surpasses anything in this life that it is "very much better." It's as though Paul could find no superlative adequate to express the comparison between being on earth and being with Christ in heaven.

E. The Need to Remain (vv. 24-26)

1. Its necessity (vv. 24-25)

"To remain on in the flesh is more necessary for your sake. And convinced of this I know that I shall remain and continue with you all for your progress and joy in the faith."

One mark of a spiritual man is that his own desires are balanced by the needs of others. That's the kind of man who could write, "Do nothing from selfishness or empty conceit, but with humility of mind let each of you regard one another as more important than himself; do not merely look out for your own personal interests, but also for the interests of others" (Phil. 2:3-4).

The Philippians needed Paul. Philippians 2:1-4 indicates they needed to learn humility. Chapter 3 implies they were imperiled by the Judaizers. In 4:1-3 Paul had to deal with contentious women in the Philippian church. The Philippians needed to be reminded to rejoice and be content in their circumstances. And the Philippians were only one of many churches that Paul believed needed him (cf. 2 Cor. 11:28).

Paul knew the churches needed him so badly that their need was likely to determine his future: "Convinced [or, confident] of this, I know that I shall remain and continue with you all for your progress and joy in the faith" (v. 25). I think that expresses Paul's conviction concerning his future—not a revelation that he was going to remain on earth. That's because if he had received a revelation, he probably would have said so, thus alleviating his friends' concern that he might be sentenced to death by the emperor. In Acts 27:21-26 Paul received a supernatural revelation that though the ship he was on would sink, the lives of all on board would be spared. He relayed that information to allay the fear of the crew, and I think he would have done the same here.

Paul was convinced that he would *menō* (remain) and *paramenō* (continue or come alongside)—a play on words. He would remain for the purpose of aiding the Philippians' spiritual "progress and joy in the faith" (v. 25). "Progress" (Gk., *prokopē*) pictures blazing a trail for the advance of an army. By remaining, Paul expected to blaze a trail for the Philippians to follow on to victory. Their faith in Christ would increase, thus leading to an increase in their joy.

2. Its purpose (v. 26)

"So that your proud confidence in me may abound in Christ Jesus through my coming to you again."

That verse begins with the Greek word *hina*, which when combined with a verb stated in the subjunctive mood ("may abound") indicates the writer is introducing a statement of purpose or explaining a reason. It is best translated, "In order that your proud confidence may abound in Christ Jesus in me." Whereas the *New American Standard* places the words "in me" before "in Christ Jesus," the Greek New Testament has "in Christ Jesus" first. It's important that the Greek word order be preserved so it doesn't sound like Paul said, "That your proud confidence in me may abound"—something Paul never would have written. His point was not that the Philippians' confidence would overflow because of him, but because of Christ's working in him.

Conclusion

Although Paul desired to be with Christ in heaven, he also wanted to remain on earth to help strengthen the church. He knew that if he stayed the church would better glorify Christ, and glorifying Christ was all he desired.

The natural question after reading Paul's great testimony is, What happened to him? Most likely he was released shortly before the burning of Rome in A.D. 64 (for which Emperor Nero falsely blamed the Christians). He was imprisoned again and beheaded sometime between A.D. 65-67. During the time of his freedom before his final imprisonment and execution, he helped many churches. Paul's assurance of release as expressed in Philippians 1:25-26 proved to be correct.

Philippians 2:19-23 indicates Paul intended to send Timothy to Philippi with the news of his release, and apparently he did so. He began a journey to Asia Minor, and on the way left Titus on the island of Crete to set the churches there in order and appoint leaders (Titus 1:5). He then apparently went on to Ephesus, traveled to Colosse (Philem. 22), and returned to Ephesus.

Upon his return to Ephesus he met Timothy, who brought news from Philippi. While at Ephesus Paul removed from leadership two of the worst leaders in the church, Hymenaeus and Alexander (1 Tim. 1:20), and left Timothy in charge. He went on to Macedonia as he had planned (Phil. 2:24; 1 Tim. 1:3) and from there wrote to Timothy with instructions and encouragement for the task of setting things in order in Ephesus (cf. 1 Tim. 3:14-15).

Paul also wrote to Titus from Macedonia, asking Titus to meet him in Nicopolis, which is on the west coast of Greece. Paul apparently spent the winter there with him (Titus 3:12) and then left for Asia Minor, leaving Trophimus sick at Miletus (2 Tim. 4:20). He may also have said a final, tearful good-bye to Timothy there (2 Tim. 1:4). He then traveled to Troas and visited Carpus (2 Tim. 4:13).

It may be that in Troas Paul was arrested for the second time—in any event he was soon arrested. He was again taken to Rome and imprisoned briefly under severe conditions, with only Luke there to comfort him (2 Tim. 4:11). Demas forsook him, and the rest of his friends were elsewhere (v. 10). From Rome he wrote his last epistle, urging Timothy to come to him and bring Mark along as well (vv. 9, 11). He was staring death in the face, and we don't know whether they were able to get to Rome before Paul's execution.

After his first imprisonment God gave Paul a few more years for fruitful ministry. He fully lived for Christ. That's all that ought to matter to us. It doesn't matter what trouble we're in or what detractors we have—even if we're facing death. What's important is that Christ is glorified and His kingdom is advanced. Paul's example is a pattern for us as we grow in Christ and seek to honor Him.

Focusing on the Facts

1. How was Adoniram Judson like Paul (see pp. 47-48)?
2. What did Paul mean by the phrase "live on in the flesh" (Phil. 1:22; see p. 49)?
3. What did Paul expect if he lived on in the physical world (see p. 49)?
4. As used in Philippians 1:22, what does the Greek word *ergon* refer to (see p. 50)?
5. What did the author of Psalm 71 and King Hezekiah share in common with Paul (see pp. 50-51)?
6. True or false: The choice of going to be with Christ in heaven or advancing Christ's kingdom on earth was an easy one for Paul (see p. 51).
7. How does the Greek verb *sunechō* picture Paul's choice of whether to be with Christ in heaven or advance His kingdom on earth (see p. 52)?
8. How does the desire of Greek philosophers differ from the desire Paul expresses in Philippians 1:23 (see pp. 52-53)?
9. Where does a believer go when he leaves this world? Support your answer with Scripture (see p. 53).
10. One mark of a spiritual man is that his own desires are balanced by the _____ ___ _____ (see p. 54).
11. Why did the Philippians need Paul (see p. 54)?
12. What was Paul confident of? Explain (Phil. 1:25; see pp. 54-55).
13. What does the Greek word translated "progress" depict that Paul expected to do for the Philippians (see p. 55)?
14. What did Paul want the Philippians to be confident of (Phil. 1:26; see p. 55)?

Pondering the Principles

1. Paul's great desire was to serve and glorify God, wherever that might be and whatever the cost to himself. Yet such singlemindedness often characterizes those building earthly kingdoms more than those who ought to be building God's kingdom. Puritan Thomas Brooks said, "Be ashamed, Christians, that worldlings are more studious and industrious to make sure of pebbles, than you are to make sure of pearls" (*The Golden Treasury of Puritan Quotations*, ed. I.D.E. Thomas [Edinburgh: Banner of

Truth Trust, 1977], p. 258). Is your life given to serving and glorifying God in contrast to the way that so many in this world are given to serving and glorifying themselves?

2. Philippians 1:12-26 portrays a man content to be where God placed him. He was equally willing to go and be with Christ or stay and serve the needs of Christ's church. That's because Paul's heart and mind were set on heaven and fulfilling the desires of heaven's Master; his contentment was a by-product of his focus. Yet often we find ourselves discouraged and discontent because of our circumstances. Thomas Watson wrote, "Spiritual things satisfy; the more of heaven is in us, the less earth will content us. . . . Fly aloft in your affections, thirst after the graces and comforts of the Spirit; the eagle that flies above in the air, fears not the stinging of the serpent; the serpent creeps on his belly, and stings only such creatures as go upon the earth" (*The Art of Divine Contentment* [Glasgow: Free Presbyterian Publications, n.d.], pp. 97-98). Consider what your heart and mind are set on. If they're set on the right things, you'll be content with the circumstances in which God has placed you.

Scripture Index

2 Samuel
24:14 — 52

Job
13:16 — 38
19:26 — 38

Psalms
22:4-5 — 39
22:8 — 39
25:2-3 — 41
31:1 — 39
33:18-19 — 39
34:7 — 39
35:25-27 — 41
40:15-16 — 41
41:1 — 39
51:12 — 8
69:6-7 — 41
71:17-18 — 50
119:80 — 41

Isaiah
1:27-29 — 41
38:18-19 — 51
45:14-17 — 41
49:23 — 41-42
50:7 — 41

Jeremiah
12:13 — 41

Zephaniah
3:11 — 41

Zechariah
4:6 — 40

Matthew
10:32 — 41

Luke
9:23 — 37
14:27 — 37

John
14:16 — 40
14:26 — 40
16:13 — 40
16:33 — 8

Acts
1:8 — 40
7:59-60 — 53
9:15 — 41
9:26 — 36
17:10-11 — 22
20:23-24 — 43
20:24 — 13
21:13 — 43
22:14-15 — 41
26:29 — 14
27:21-26 — 54
28:16-31 — 9-10
28:20 — 14
28:22 — 17
28:23-24 — 16
28:30-31 — 16

Romans
1:10 — 8
1:11 — 8
1:13 — 12, 50
1:15 — 13
1:29 — 30
8:5 — 49
8:9 — 40
8:26 — 40
8:28 — 38, 40
9:1-3 — 36
9:33 — 42

15:23	8	1:14	16-18, 24-25
15:24	8	1:15	25-27
15:30	39	1:15-18	22
		1:16	13, 27-28
1 Corinthians		1:17	28-30
9:16	13	1:18	7, 23, 30-31
10:1	12	1:19	37-41
12:1	12	1:20	39, 41-42
13:1-2	28	1:21	42-44, 48-49
16:15	50	1:22	49-52
		1:22-26	48
2 Corinthians		1:23	52-54
5:6-8	53	1:23-24	42, 52
5:8	52	1:24-25	54-55
6:10	36	1:25-26	56
10:3	49	1:26	55
11:4	25	1:26-27	50
11:23-28	36	1:27	13
11:28	54	2:1-4	54
12:20	30	2:3	28-29
		2:17	11
Galatians		2:19-23	56
1:6	25	2:20	27, 36
2:20	49	2:24	56
5:16-17	49	2:25-30	11
5:20-21	30	2:30	50
5:22	8, 41, 50	3:1	11-12
5:25	49	3:13	12
		4:1	12
Ephesians		4:1-3	54
3:20	41	4:4	8, 11
6:18-19	39	4:18-19	11
6:20	14	4:22	14
Philippians		**1 Thessalonians**	
1:3-4	11	4:13	12
1:5	13	5:10	53
1:7	9, 13	5:16	8
1:11	50	5:25	39
1:12	11-13		
1:12-26	7, 58	**1 Timothy**	
1:13	13-16	1:3	56

1:20	56	Philemon	
3:14-15	56	22	56
6:4	30		
		Hebrews	
2 Timothy		13:15	50
1:4	56		
1:15	27, 36	James	
4:6	52	1:2-3	8
4:9-11	56		
4:10	36, 56	1 Peter	
4:13	55	4:2	49
4:16	27	5:2	29
4:20	56	5:3	29
Titus		3 John	
1:5	56	9	29
3:12	56		

Topical Index

Accusations, false. *See* Detractors

Barclay, William
  on "hard-pressed" in Philippians 1:23, 52
  on "progress" in Philippians 1:12, 13
Boldness, lack of, 16-17
Bridges, Jerry, on patience vs. revenge, 32
Brooks, Thomas, on Christians not being as diligent as the worldly, 57-58

Circumstances. *See* Trials

Daille, John, on God's using preachers with bad motives, 31
Death
  deliverance from, 37-39
  fate of Christians immediately following, 53
  joy in spite of, 11, 35-46
Deliverance, from death. *See* Death
Detractors, joy in spite of, 11, 21-33

Eadie, John, on the power of the gospel, 30
Evangelism
  furthering the gospel, 11-16, 31-32
  on the job, 16
  motives behind, 30-31

False teachers. *See* Detractors

Flesh, the
  definition of, 49
  joy in spite of, 11, 57-58

Gospel, furthering the. *See* Evangelism

Hamlet's musings about suicide vs. Paul, 43
Happiness. *See* Joy
Heaven
  confidence in the promise of, 41-42
  earth vs., 51-55
Holy Spirit, provision of the, 40-41

Jealousy, in ministry. *See* Detractors
Joy
  in ministry, 7
  in spite of death (*see* Death)
  in spite of detractors (*see* Detractors)
  in spite of the flesh (*see* Flesh)
  in spite of trouble (*see* Trials)
Judson, Adoniram, ministry of, 47-49
Justice, preoccupation with, 32

MacArthur, John, what most discourages him in ministry, 22
Manton, Thomas
  on joy that can't be touched, 19
  on vindication from slander, 23

Meyer, F. B., Paul's witness to the praetorian guard, 15-16
Ministry
  desire for, 50-56
  detractors in (*see* Detractors)
  diligence in, 57-58
  discouragements in, 22
  joy of, 7
  trust required for, 22-23
  work of the 49-50
Motivation, object of, 13

Paul
  detractors against, 21-33
  evangelism among the praetorian guard, 14-16
  final years of, 55-56
  imprisonment of, 8-18, 55-56
  joy of, 7-58
  sufferings of, 35-36
  supporters of, 27-28
Prayer, confidence in, 39

Revenge, not seeking, 32
Ryle, J. C., on the excellence of the Christian battle, 45

Selfishness, in ministry. *See* Detractors

Shakespeare, William, on Hamlet's musings about suicide, 43
Simeon, Charles, on designs against pious ministers by jealous men, 24
Slander, in ministry. *See* Detractors
Soul sleep, refuting the notion of, 53
Suicide, Hamlet vs. Paul, 43

Tozer, A. W., on Christian happiness, 45
Trials, joy in spite of, 7-19, 44-45, 58
Trust, in ministry. *See* Ministry

Vengeance. *See* Revenge
Vindication, against detractors. *See* Detractors

Watson, Thomas
  on spiritual joy, 19
  on spiritual satisfaction, 58
Will of God, confidence in the, 42

Moody Press, a ministry of the Moody Bible Institute,
is designed for education, evangelization, and edification.
If we may assist you in knowing more about Christ
and the Christian life, please write us without obligation:
Moody Press, c/o MLM, Chicago, Illinois 60610.